VEHEMENCE

INTENSITY OF FEELING

SADIYA AHMED

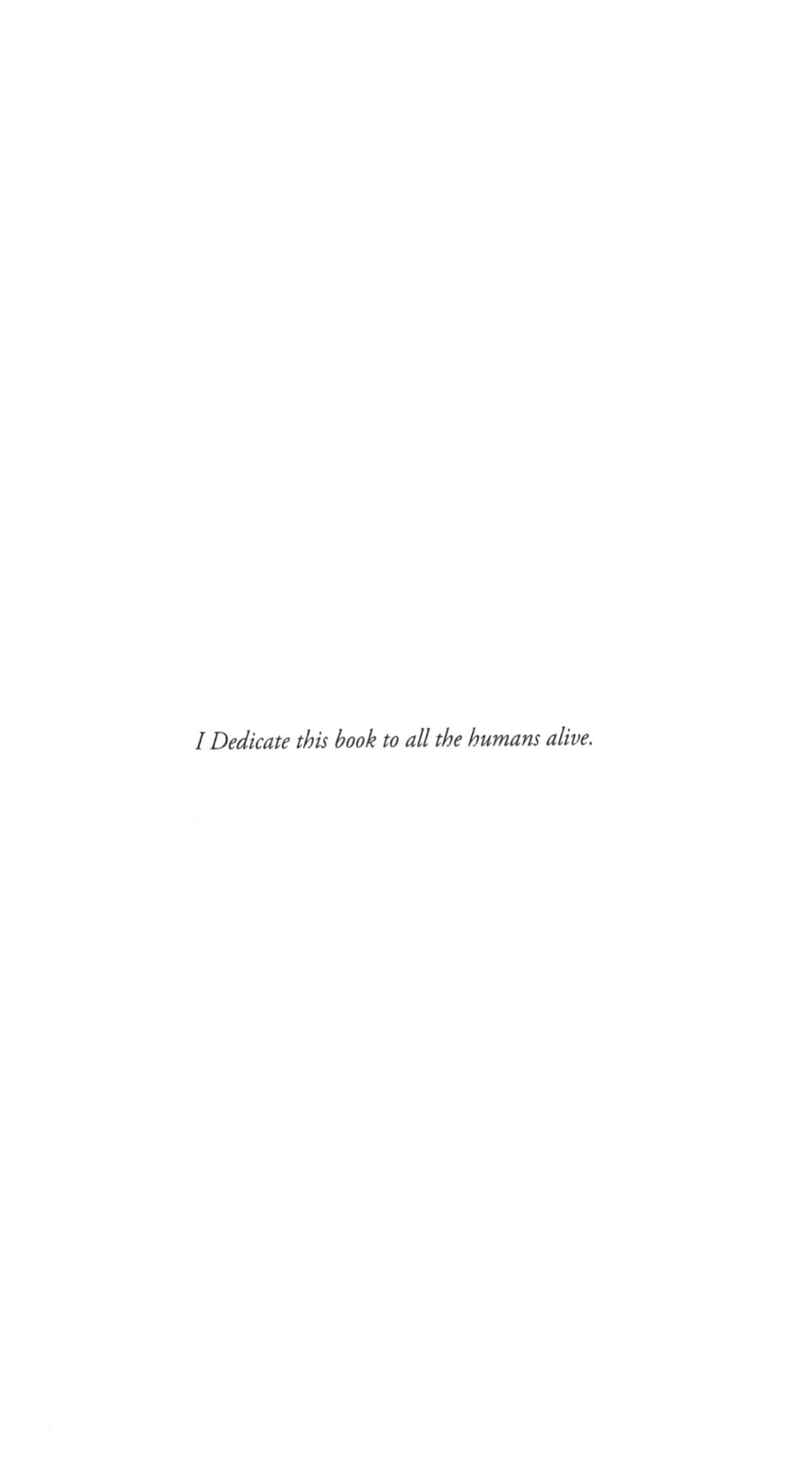

I Dedicate this book to all the humans alive.

Contents

Contents

Contents

Acknowledgements

Dear, Era

Thankyou for reading my words again and again . I understand how annoying it can be but you know you are my personal corrector.

I served your kingdom my whole life and I swear, my offspring will

do the same.

- The Rose

VEHEMENCE

intensity of feeling

to pen down words is easy but to pen down emotions is
hallelujah...

Chapter1

there is a specific melody
that rings in every mind
without word.
- S.Ahmed

Chapter2

isn't it beautiful
how sacred life is
we think we got infinite time
but what we have is only a few seconds
because every breath that we take lasts for a few seconds
and again begin with zero.
- S.Ahmed

Chapter3

i'm a prisoner
inside this body of clay and water.
-S.Ahmed

Chapter4

With eyes closed
I peeled the layers of my memories
Stopped, when I saw colors around me Colors of joy.
Yellow... Yellow is so bright
That I can feel summer around me when it's actually winter .
Looking up at the sky so blue with clouds like cotton.
Grass tickled my feet As I slowly opened my eyes,
with thoughts in my mind How did I forget.
when you mix all the colours it becomes grey.
S.Ahmed

Chapter5

Seeing the world from apart
looks delightful
but I start wandering around the alleys
I got to see grave
No wonder why all and sundry bury
but little did I know
what's cooking into the abyss
little did I know what's obvious.
-S.Ahmed

Chapter6

The world will seem beautiful
when looked by An insane mind.
-S.Ahmed

Chapter7

A chill ran down my spine

When I witness my deepest fear

in front of my eyes

It felt like it's a dream come true,

which I've been hiding in the depth of my mind

Losing what I treasure the most

is just like Gollum losing its precious

The more I try to hold you in my hand

The more rapidly I am losing

your nature is sand

that I have never realised

You are my time which I can never hold in my grip so,

let me be your sea

beause I am aware that one day you'll drown.

- S.Ahmed

Chapter8

The world will seem

when looked by An insane mind.

-S.Ahmed

Chapter9

Love is either the beginning
or the end of mysterious shit.
-S.Ahmed

Chapter10

A Serene felling inside my pump
All I can hear is my beating heart so calm
whatever it is I'm not aware
But something feels off
suddenly all I can hear is my beating heart
Do you know what it is?
Because I'm not aware of the silence before the storm.
A Serene felling inside my pump
All I can hear is my beating heart so calm.
-S.Ahmed

Chapter11

When I look up at the sky I wonder,
how sacred the universe is
We are standing on the different land
But gazing the same sky.
-S.Ahmed

Chapter12

And here Comes October with fall.
Who would have thought that fall can be beautiful,
mesmerizing but it is...
It's that time of the year
When sun starts to feel cozy ,
When there Is a hint of chill in the air
with wicked shapes of cloud in the Sky stealing the limelight .
And the leaves, oh the leaves turning yellow,
Sending happiness as they reach the ground telling us
No matter how high you are
you'll meet the ground for sure,
And here comes October with fall.
-S.Ahmed

Chapter13

If only we know how to love

Without pride and prejudice.

Then love will be Serene.

-S.Ahmed

Chapter14

Clouds in the sky
resemble the thoughts in our mind
Both changes perpetually from one to another.
-S.Ahmed

Chapter15

A melody of old in my ear

A hint of smile on my lips

As the sun kissed my skin

With a touch of warmth

Tears filling the eyes

As the memory of you emerging in mind.

- S.Ahmed

Chapter16

Someone's love,

Lost in the sky.

Reaching the sea shore

where Someone's else love is getting lost in the sea.

-S.Ahmed

Chapter17

Shore is nowhere in sight
But the end is
Left, Right, Left. I marched,
but the more I marched forward
the end does the same
Trapped in the loop
With no hope for the shore
But still I marched forward
In the hope for the shore.
- S.Ahmed

Chapter18

I am caught in time
So does my mind.
I might seem I'm here,
in front of your naked eye
But I'm not
because I'm caught in time.
- S,Ahmed

Chapter19

As the mist wrapped this mesmerizing sight

It started to get cold

Spring is treasured

Goosebumps are staying longer than expected

Warmth is nowhere in sight

Feet are as cold as ice

Cheeks are flushed red

So does the winter is hear.

- S.Ahmed

Chapter20

And I'm nothing but a myth
You created with the power of imagination.
-S.Ahmed

Chapter21

And I remember what I saw in that alley .

A tree, a tree without it's green,

Somehow managing to support a life on its high

A life of another species.

you are not a waste as you think you are, because you are not aware of what role you have been alloted since the day you are born.

- S.Ahmed

Chapter22

Let me touch this coldness

Let my hand touch the air

Let my skin deliver this message to my soul,

that how cold the outside world has become.

- S.Ahmed

Chapter23

And when I was lost in the depth of my mind

All I can see is death,

With a little bit of life.

Like that person laying on the death bed,

With a little bit of life.

I can see the dead green with blossom on it.

I can see the man fighting for the air.

If only the will to live is strong you can see life in every dead.

**because even a dead becomes a fertilizer.*

- S.Ahmed

Chapter24

How am I supposed to forget
when my soul Smells like you.
- S.Ahmed

Chapter25

Through my window

I have admired you blooming in every freezing winter .

You were so red. Like a new born baby's blush.

I have watched you changing colors,

From green to yellow.

I have watched you shedding leaves

And blooming flowers.

And off course sprinkling cotton in the air.

But I haven't realized You are aging.

Until one day when you didn't bloom.

I have been waiting to see you bloom those beautiful flowers.

But I didn't realized You are long gone ,

because you were still. Standing high among those greens,

that made me believe,

You will bloom again red, so red.

- S.Ahmed

Chapter26

If only I know
You will dissolve in the fine dust
I've embraced you even more.
-S.Ahmed

Chapter27

Darkness is what will be treasured

Because even the moon has left.

- S.Ahmed

Chapter28

I pity the daylight
Because only the darkness knows,
How pretty the stars are.
- S,Ahmed

Chapter29

Laying on the death bed
Somehow managing to take breath
With the help of tools.
I got to understand the value of life.
Hanging on the cliff,
I heald the rope as thin as the thread ,
Tight as I can with my dying hands.
Probability playing tricks in my mind.
Who will win?
My will to live or the eater of soul.
Because I'm on the verge of demise.
- S.Ahmed

Chapter30

With my conscious mind
I let it touched my lips,
And run through my veins
Reaching the conscious mind.
Waiting for it's magic to begin.
And as it begins,
I feel the weight lift off my shoulders
Making me feel like cotton.
I am under its spell and I'm well aware of the fact.
- S.Ahmed

Chapter31

It's a pure bliss

When you are Under the sin's Spell.

- S.Ahmed

Chapter32

As I have committed a sin

I'm afraid what will happen to this body of clay and water

When my soul leaves to reunite with its

Body In the land of judgment.

- S.Ahmed

Chapter33

As I stood beside a living

On the verge of demise.

I felt like I'm drowning into the pool of my Sins.

I can feel the fear building in the pit of my stomach

But I shall not call it fear Because at that moment I wasn't afraid of my doings.

What I am actually afraid is to face the reality.

- S.Ahmed

Chapter34

I feel ashamed,

Because this body of clay and water is moving like it was supposed to.

My lips reciting the hymn like they were taught

If you'll se me you'll praise me.

But oh man! You are so wrong

Because my body is just doing what it was taught

And it's only me

who knows that I didn't feel connected to the almighty At that moment

but when I do, I can see all my Sins in front of my naked eyes.

And I can't stop my tears Because I feel ashamed.

And deep down I know I'll be doing it again and again

And I'll be standing in front of the almighty

Begging for forgiveness Again and again.

- S.Ahmed

Chapter35

As Time flew by

The moon is filling itself With it's lost self

In the presence of the sun.

-S.Ahmed

Chapter36

As the sun sets
It bleeds all the possible colors
Just to make itself remembered.
-S.Ahmed

Chapter37

To,
The sun I'll be needing you even more
To keep me alive in this freezing winter .
- S.Ahmed

Chapter38

If I ever fall into the parallel universe

Will I be with you?

Will the sun show me the same flames?

Or I'll be walking in the moonlight In search of a way back

home.

- S.Ahmed

Chapter39

It's ravishing how you look
When the sky is on fire.
-S.Ahmed

Chapter40

Where are you my beloved Or shall I say my other half?

I've heard that, I am made with a certain part Of your body.

Probably the Rib.

Where are you my beloved?

It's been decades, I've been longing for you.

Where are you my beloved?

Because all I know,

Is that we are made in pairs,

And I'm a part of your body.

- S.Ahmed

Chapter41

And I'll always look at you with the same Same grace

In my eyes

As I did when my heart was dancing.

-S.Ahmed

Chapter42

He asked me do I believe in destiny?

I was confused should I say yes or stay silent.

Because my whole life I believed in.

But in that moment I had a doubt.

Is it really destiny that we met, I asked my subconscious.

Because if it is not Then what it is?

- S.Ahmed

Chapter43

You'll always be alive
In people's memory.
The dead will be remembered.
- S.Ahmed

Chapter44

A human in his life will never achieve True satisfaction.
Because a human mind will always craves for more
And as it reaches its desire.
The urge for more will be soon planted instead brain.
By our nafs.

- S.Ahmed

Chapter45

I begin a journey with the unfamiliar faces
and as the Time for my departure is coming closer
I'm getting familiar with these faces.
- S.Ahmed

Chapter46

In the way
I stood there watching people come and go
while I'm waiting for my time to arrive...
the time when I'll be reunited with the almighty.
- S.Ahmed

Chapter47

Desire has been planted
In your system from the day
You were born.
- S.Ahmed

Chapter48

Nothing in this world
can be pushed Upon you, it's all your will.
- S.Ahmed

Chapter49

Happiness is just for a mere moment,

So enjoy it because sadness is what's treasured.

- S.Ahmed

Chapter50

They say you are born alone
And you'll die alone.
So why do you seek love, Or a companion.
When you are already aware of the reality?
-S.Ahmed

Chapter51

Oh my beloved don't get lost in the beauty of this world,
because it's nothing but a rat trap.
You shall seek because you will return.
- S.Ahmed

Chapter52

A day had been destined

When this body of clay and water will return home.

- S.Ahmed

Chapter53

We all are puppets
Just with different master.
- S.Ahmed

Author's Note

Hello beautiful readers, I hope this book finds you in the best moment of your life. This book *VEHEMENCE intensity of feeling* is my first book.

You can find me on istagram as thoughts_inyourbrain.